A Delighted Bat

BY J.C. DOWDY

A DELIGHTED BAT

This book is written to provide information and motivation to readers. Its purpose is not to render any type of psychological, legal, or professional advice of any kind. The content is the sole opinion and expression of the author, and not necessarily that of the publisher.

Copyright © 2019 by J.C. Dowdy

All rights reserved. No part of this book may be reproduced, transmitted, or distributed in any form by any means, including, but not limited to, recording, photocopying, or taking screenshots of parts of the book, without prior written permission from the author or the publisher. Brief quotations for noncommercial purposes, such as book reviews, permitted by Fair Use of the U.S. Copyright Law, are allowed without written permissions, as long as such quotations do not cause damage to the book's commercial value. For permissions, write to the publisher, whose address is stated below.

Printed in the United States of America.

ISBN   978-1-64552-055-9   (Paperback)
ISBN   978-1-64552-056-6   (Digital)

Lettra Press books may be ordered through booksellers or by contacting:

Lettra Press LLC
18229 E 52nd Ave.
Denver City, CO 80249
1 303 586 1431 | info@lettrapress.com
www.lettrapress.com

Dedications

In loving memory of my Mother and Father: Jack B. Dowdy and Madie Jo Dowdy

In memory of my best friend, Gaylon Gary

In fond and loving memory of Dr. Selma L. Bishop. The greatest educator who ever lived, my poetry teacher and friend.

My sister, Jan Canada and Brother-in-Law, Rick Canada

Thany-you Jan for being yourself, and a Nurse! Don't forget, I love you more!

My nephew, Arron Mazon, his wife, Kris, and their beautiful daughters, Nicole, Haley, and Emily.

My nephew, Jon Canada, his wife, Brie, and their beautiful children, Cadence And Jack.

My aunt Bobby Haines, a true Texas Rancher, and Lady. We love you, Bobby!

Best friend from the Navy and life, Ira Dube.

Robby Brewer, the best builder and friend in West Texas.

Brad Bratton, a friend since childhood, a king of friends, thank-you Brad.

Michele {McGurk} Drake and husband Rick Drake. Michele, a friend since
Sicily and now forever!

My beautiful wife, Juana Dowdy. When I met you in the Rep. of Panama I knew
you were the one. My little Cuna Indian, I Love You.

About The Book

I'm very proud of this little book, not for being a few of my favorite poems, but for the unique circumstances I found myself in while composing them. A few were written while serving in the U.S. Marine Corps, others with the U.S. Navy.

The title, {A Delighted Bat} springs from these two reasons: 1. A bat's ability to detect through echo sound. 2. Bats pollinate. While in Panama, I swatted a bat, gently placed him outside my compound's screen window ledge, and behold, the little guy reappeared twice! He realized I meant him no real harm; he only wanted to say thank-you.

Now here is my analogy: A reader will detect through sound, one or more meanings of her or his own, pollinating a distinct philosophy and make the poem of choice their own. Makes sense to me. I do it.

A few poems may appear esoteric, well, act like a bat, avoid the wall, find your roost, and make your words your home, these poems belong to you now.

About The Author

I was born in Sinton, Texas, raised in San Angelo and Abilene, Texas. During my school years. I found my views on school a bit radical, never protesting outside myself about it. I don't know why.

I had friends, good friends and best friends. I loved girls, they always seemed more mature about life, schools and relationships.

They certainly outclassed me.

My parents were a gift, a special gift, never once did I hear or see them judge or treat others badly, and they listened to me, they cared and respected both myself and my sister's opinions.

I often wondered how I deserved them...still a mystery.

I had always loved to read the encyclopedias and varied dictionaries my parents bought me, {I just gave my age away} I found peace between those pages. I quit school when I turned sixteen, studied poetry under Dr. Selma L. Bishop, joined the U.S. Marine Corps at seventeen. All the while I wrote.

I realize one's life cannot be summarized in a few words; forgive my curtness. I hope to hear from whomever reads my little book.

Everyone has a story.

Symbols

The Rhodesian Man, with similar simian friend Neanderthal, discuss the nature of the "Rose" near Gethsamane.

Rhodesian Man: I choose not to waiver ignorance. the most sublime of tranquilities, the mate of "Humility's
Romance", when I refer to the rose as youth,
it's thorns as guardians of pride, protecting it's colors
which rudely divide, Nature's pose of harmony.
what say you Neanderthal?

Neanderthal: Her parentage surely knew of harm, having any shield to protect against claims her petals
carry potent charms; the prickles she bears shout revenge! A prelude of defense it seems, should she perish, would her aroma linger within the future hearts
of "Man", or will her formation change as calendars fall,
shedding her sweetness, decaying the stem fermenting
her call?

Rhodesian Man: I soundly denounce this tryst with the rose!
Curiosity has leveled my ignorant role, has planted thistles,
imparing my stance with "Humility's Romance"..
no arborescent form from any simple norm, should shatter
this garden I've grown, only "Man" truly withers never
to return, while this plant, this plant returns!

Neanderthal: My friend, the similarities and differences
which descend upon us are artificial, truth is flourished
through events, not speculations, to say logic will kiss
a belief and subdue it's myth, "tis only a clue,
should the tundra yield and swallow this field, the "Rose"
shall remain, and the truth, not the lies will live,
I believe this belief to be real.

Lead Me Astray

Wendy, lead me astray
Along some foreign shore,
Of a poet's favorite dream,
Where two exotic suns
Coat a pyramid and two grey
Pylons sing, come, come closer,
Relieve our domains,
Experience in touch,
Feel what few have seen.

Melancholia Insomnia

The clown revealed himself in parts,
Laughed with the crowd,
Then tearfully departed;
Leaving the loud, the commonly sane,
And the many laughing,
Who never knew…
"The Cane of Man" is but a child's
Frailty, and we are the makers
Of it's ill use.

Alexandria

Egypt by way of sea,
Seems a slightly smaller
Scene to me, until the docking
Ignited expectations which experience
Detests and explains:

"Careful must your eyes perceive
This beauty dawned by night, illusions
Are fragile, nontransparent toys when sight
Lies distant from delight.

Alexandria! Behold this once cultured
City now drained by "TIME AND MAN",
Stretching Her ruins to Cairo, marking
"Infinity's Ecstasy", which time compelled
To stray, a berthing for the peasant's prey.

I blame not technology for the advancement
On poverty, or myself, having not secured
A wave from reaching shore, I can see
The shattered whole, the pieces thrown,
And though each fragment is less than
That originally known, the final picture is fair,
Especially before the pushing of that wave,
And experience drawn.

A Silent Study

Author's Note: I use the word "Epigenesis" loosely, I prefer it being associated with my idea of being. Philosophy tries to uproot one's worth; in this poem, mine.

A Silent Study

Awake my Epigenesis!
We are here to learn and share
Motionless you may appear,
Through you conquer not through
Stride,
Still, I miss all which happens
Here.

Awake my Epigenesis!
If many symbolizes common,
And uncommon crystallizes few,
Which one are you my Epigenesis?

The simple often trampled grass
Is seldom seen,
Where lies the splinter
Crushed,
Yet untouched?

I lose all in glance at man-kind
And gain little through whispers
Noticed;
What fate bestows
You, my Epigenesis, as one
Unnoticed?

Should I lose a friend
As you, my breath shall cease
To hold this body this mind
Claims dear…

Awake my Epigenesis!
If all relevant
The beauty is of unity,
And we must surely live as one

An Excerpt From Exasperation

You shed no light on such
matters, age is trivial to this heart
so finely undermanned; bountiful
care for lesser creatures endowed
by simple knowledge have I healed,
never having touched a soul; to wreath
a mind of inferior kind by wrath
of speech, lingers within my reach,
To touch a mortal entity never known
sings a wake, a knelling sound
shattering to my hope..surely a
stranger jest has played upon a bigger
fool than you!

I have neither carried or attempted
to carry this side of "Man" which
irritates many like you. To murder
this exposed side is meant for no
resurrection of a twin; I bear no other
"Man's" trivial cannonized beliefs that
wars this designed planet, nor do I
partake in another's festivities for life;

The Tradition's Enemy

Christmas! Shoppers greeted the sun,
Reflecting their spirits as curious sprites,
Gathering an hopeful glance at tradition;
Viva! Viva! The "Tradition Hunters" sang,
In unison, as told to them before their time
By a lesson from a hawk teaching praise.
Traditions carry many faults of yesteryear,
As oxygen is useless without "God's creations,
Or as the closed mind of a war-like human,
Sleeping with a sinister's skill, until his youth
Taught his life, that the gifted feelings deserve
More for demanding nothing.

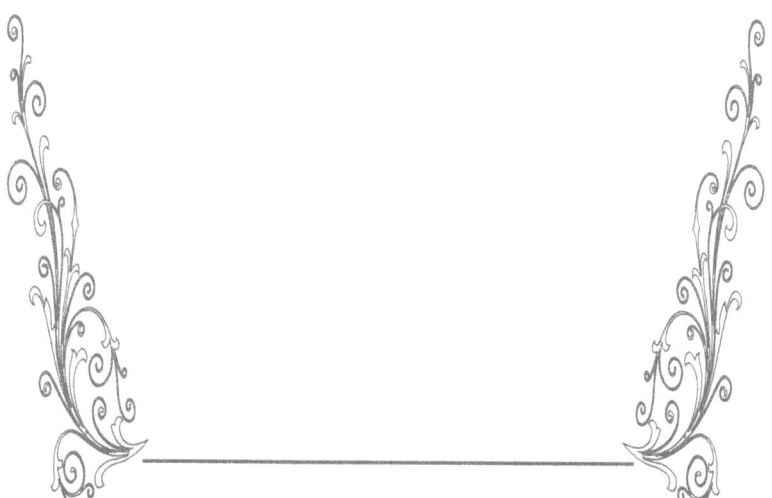

The Elf

Author's Note: While egos are distorted and rearranged
according to substance taken, all cares
are casted to and fro, only to be mistaken
by the world from which they came.
The Elf
An entangled matter of strange mangled
minds form elusive identities,
each working for the other-self
quoting passages from their elf.

Within this thought as sought never before
by manner of will, importance, or possession,
detained by mortality, a loose haughty
breeze, whispers to one's self…

Gather your wants and needs, each matters
not, I am fore-known to be;
your substance is mine alone to choose,
it has been brought to you by me.

When truth reveals my awakening,
your days and nights belong to all
around and close to you, I will shatter
knowledge, obstruct memory, and send
your lambs to my butcher for cost.

Screaming calls share themselves with your elf,
a reminder of who left what behind,
chanting timelessly.."Though memory is short
during my stay, memory is long
through experience.
I am the Elf, I am your Elf!

Within My Rotunda

{Paraphrasing an event}

A secret façade screams for me,
While two skeptics peer through
My door with sighs of awe,
One spirit still, the other in motion
Within my rotunda, on no small pittance
Of mine.

One lighted silhouette streamed solely
Toward me by no directed thought,
My unknown painter captured my feature
Capturing light around my rotunda
So morbid in sequence of day.

The other intrinsic being of spectral kind,
Not bounded by time or sepulcher,
Waved solemnly for me to follow
From my somber state into a region
Of it's own away from my rotunda.

A sheet of force from hands unseen
Soured even more my emotions,
When slay not me they disagreed,
Holding me spatial for seconds,
Then let me alone to a new world
Within my rotunda.

Wishful Words

The furrow was planted with seeds,
Known and grown by him only,
The ground was only fertile for weeds,
Still he persisted to grow
His one lonely flower.

Being not a classicist, he vowed
To produce a flower not found
In other lands, but a plant which
Would induce a more natural
Scent for our hour.

He hitch-hiked through {new school}
Thought and found a range among a few
With heart, an ineffaceable fact
That bored into a soul without
Sound or tower.

Come winter the seeds had died,
Frail skin dried, and the art
Or planting too.
The remaining seasons marked an age
That tried to make the earth sound,
Still the soil was sour.

Endings never tell how hard he tried.

The Augus-Eyed Wanderer

If ugliness is beauty stained by thought,
Is this not so if I see this?

Is life such a silent lot of work, marriage,
children, a yard with tree symbolizing growth
and nothing more?

The Drawing Room

She before me sat quite elegantly,
Singing words into phrases without hint.
Caring not for starvation, I silently awaited
My dessert, for the art of listening sights
The gift for speaking.

Youth to aging toppled heights surprising,
As she uttered these never feigning words:
"Stentorian patterns dwell beyond seasonal
Wintry effects, shining no dimmer light on age,
When accounting acts from youth…
Youth is common to the old, you know".

I visioned her as Venus without control,
Enlightening my soul to heights a philter
Might impose, a versifer waning not,
Gaining universal trend through a verbal sit.
Knowingly, my captured being subsided.

If love were matter, not feeling, how careful
Might I embrace this storm of angelic form?

Sinedie

No love could near my love M-Jane.
Synchronized by hour-glass fate,
Lying visavis,
We challenged destiny,
And stroked the thorn
Of three.

No love could near my love M-Jane?
Dove should fear dove
Signaling flight,
Shedding no power from pyramid
Trilogy form;
Mementoes of heart are pieced
From elegies,
We are living epitaphs
Of their charm.

Now about my love I call M-Jane;
Should finer thread dare weave
With "Humility's Skill",
Her gentle grace would roar!
Then lessen to a purr,
A softness delicate to air,
And since hushed whispers
To Tell.

Should my love M-Jane
Abandon these jaunts,
A silky science potrays
Her moods;
From lighted canvas,
This mindful kind insures,
Abstractions for the fool.

Now hear me my love M-Jane!
An antidote for portion rendered,
Allows in portion this anecdote
To survive..
Bury not a dream too far,
Or weigh a rendevous…

Alas; no love could near my love M-Jane.

www.ingramcontent.com/pod-product-compliance
Lightning Source LLC
Chambersburg PA
CBHW050613100526
44584CB00037B/2625